Thomas Hardy, A Poet In Verse

Poetry is a fascinating use of language. With almost a million words at its command it is not surprising that these Isles have produced some of the most beautiful, moving and descriptive verse through the centuries. In this series we look at poets who at first thought summon other crafts to mind.

Many giants of Literature originate from the shores of these emerald isles; Shakespeare, Dickens, Chaucer, The Brontes and Austen to which most people would willingly add the name Thomas Hardy. 'Far From The Madding Crowd',' Tess Of The D'Urbervilles', 'The Mayor Of Casterbridge' are but three of his literary masterpieces. But let us go further and add to his canon his Poems. Hardy himself thought he was a poet who wrote novels purely for the money. Indeed his poems were not published until he was in his fifties after his major novels were published and his reputation set. Today his poetry is more rightly regarded in its own right.

Many of the poems are also available as an audiobook from our sister company Portable Poetry. Many samples are at our youtube channel
http://www.youtube.com/user/PortablePoetry?feature=mhee The full volume can be purchased from iTunes, Amazon and other digital stores. Among the readers are James Taylor, Richard Mitchley and Ghizela Rowe

Index Of Poems

A Meeting With Despair
The Voice
A Thunderstorm In Town
God's Funeral
My Spirit Will Not Haunt The Mound
In The Moonlight
The Man He Killed
An August Midnight
The Dead Man Walking
Lines On The Loss Of The "Titanic"
Rome: The Vatican - Sala Delle Muse
Middle-Age Enthusiasms
Unknowing
In Vision I Roamed
"I Have Lived With Shades"
Memory And I
A Man (In Memory of H. of M.)
Mute Opinion
On An Invitation To The United States
The Tenant-For-Life
Afterwards
During Wind And Rain
The Seasons of Her Year
Heredity
He Never Expected Much
I Said To Love
I Look Into My Glass
The Subalterns

She At His Funeral
The Church-Builder
Men Who March Away
She, To Him
To An Unborn Pauper Child
The To-Be-Forgotten
In A Museum
A Confession To A Friend In Trouble
Shelley's Skylark (The neighbourhood of Leghorn: March)

A Meeting With Despair

As evening shaped I found me on a moor
Which sight could scarce sustain:
The black lean land, of featureless contour,
Was like a tract in pain.

"This scene, like my own life," I said, "is one
Where many glooms abide;
Toned by its fortune to a deadly dun
Lightless on every side.

I glanced aloft and halted, pleasure-caught
To see the contrast there:
The ray-lit clouds gleamed glory; and I thought,
"There's solace everywhere!"

Then bitter self-reproaches as I stood
I dealt me silently
As one perverse--misrepresenting Good
In graceless mutiny.

Against the horizon's dim - descernèd wheel
A form rose, strange of mould:
That he was hideous, hopeless, I could feel
Rather than could behold.

"'Tis a dead spot, where even the light lies spent
To darkness!" croaked the Thing.
"Not if you look aloft!" said I, intent
On my new reasoning.

"Yea--but await awhile!" he cried. "Ho-ho!
Look now aloft and see!"
I looked. There, too, sat night: Heaven's radiant show
Had gone. Then chuckled he.

The Voice

Woman much missed, how you call to me, call to me,
Saying that now you are not as you were

When you had changed from the one who was all to me,
But as at first, when our day was fair.

Can it be you that I hear? Let me view you, then,
Standing as when I drew near to the town
Where you would wait for me: yes, as I knew you then,
Even to the original air-blue gown!

Or is it only the breeze in its listlessness
Travelling across the wet mead to me here,
You being ever dissolved to wan wistlessness,
Heard no more again far or near?

Thus I; faltering forward,
Leaves around me falling,
Wind oozing thin through the thorn from norward,
And the woman calling.

A Thunderstorm In Town
(A Reminiscence, 1893)

She wore a 'terra-cotta' dress,
And we stayed, because of the pelting storm,
Within the hansom's dry recess,
Though the horse had stopped; yea, motionless
We sat on, snug and warm.

Then the downpour ceased, to my sharp sad pain,
And the glass that had screened our forms before
Flew up, and out she sprang to her door:
I should have kissed her if the rain
Had lasted a minute more.

God's Funeral
I saw a slowly-stepping train
Lined on the brows, scoop-eyed and bent and hoar
Following in files across a twilit plain
A strange and mystic form the foremost bore.

And by contagious throbs of thought
Or latent knowledge that within me lay
And had already stirred me, I was wrought
To consciousness of sorrow even as they.

The fore-borne shape, to my blurred eyes,
At first seemed man-like, and anon to change
To an amorphous cloud of marvellous size,
At times endowed with wings of glorious range.

And this phantasmal variousness
Ever possessed it as they drew along:
Yet throughout all it symboled none the less
Potency vast and loving-kindness strong.

Almost before I knew I bent
Towards the moving columns without a word;
They, growing in bulk and numbers as they went,
Struck out sick thoughts that could be overheard:

'O man-projected Figure, of late
Imaged as we, thy knell who shall survive?
Whence came it we were tempted to create
One whom we can no longer keep alive?

'Framing him jealous, fierce, at first,
We gave him justice as the ages rolled,
Will to bless those by circumstance accurst,
And longsuffering, and mercies manifold.

'And, tricked by our own early dream
And need of solace, we grew self-deceived,
Our making soon our maker did we deem,
And what we had imagined we believed,

'Till, in Time's stayless stealthy swing,
Uncompromising rude reality
Mangled the Monarch of our fashioning,
Who quavered, sank; and now has ceased to be.

'So, toward our myth's oblivion,
Darkling, and languid-lipped, we creep and grope
Sadlier than those who wept in Babylon,
Whose Zion was a still abiding hope.

'How sweet it was in years far hied
To start the wheels of day with trustful prayer,
To lie down liegely at the eventide
And feel a blest assurance he was there!

'And who or what shall fill his place?
Whither will wanderers turn distracted eyes
For some fixed star to stimulate their pace
Towards the goal of their enterprise?'

Some in the background then I saw,
Sweet women, youths, men, all incredulous,
Who chimed as one: 'This is figure is of straw,
This requiem mockery! Still he lives to us!'

I could not prop their faith: and yet

Many I had known: with all I sympathized;
And though struck speechless, I did not forget
That what was mourned for, I, too, once had prized.

Still, how to bear such loss I deemed
The insistent question for each animate mind,
And gazing, to my growing sight there seemed
A pale yet positive gleam low down behind,

Whereof, to lift the general night,
A certain few who stood aloof had said,
'See you upon the horizon that small light
Swelling somewhat?' Each mourner shook his head.

And they composed a crowd of whom
Some were right good, and many nigh the best
Thus dazed and puzzled 'twixt the gleam and gloom
Mechanically I followed with the rest.

My Spirit Will Not Haunt The Mound
My spirit will not haunt the mound
Above my breast,
But travel, memory-possessed,
To where my tremulous being found
Life largest, best.

My phantom-footed shape will go
When nightfall grays
Hither and thither along the ways
I and another used to know
In backward days.

And there you'll find me, if a jot
You still should care
For me, and for my curious air;
If otherwise, then I shall not,
For you, be there.

In The Moonlight
"O lonely workman, standing there
In a dream, why do you stare and stare
At her grave, as no other grave where there?"

"If your great gaunt eyes so importune
Her soul by the shine of this corpse-cold moon,
Maybe you'll raise her phantom soon!"

"Why, fool, it is what I would rather see
Than all the living folk there be;

But alas, there is no such joy for me!"

"Ah - she was one you loved, no doubt,
Through good and evil, through rain and drought,
And when she passed, all your sun went out?"

"Nay: she was the woman I did not love,
Whom all the other were ranked above,
Whom during her life I thought nothing of."

The Man He Killed
Had he and I but met
By some old ancient inn,
We should have set us down to wet
Right many a nipperkin!

But ranged as infantry,
And staring face to face,
I shot at him as he at me,
And killed him in his place.

I shot him dead because
Because he was my foe,
Just so: my foe of course he was;
That's clear enough; although

He thought he'd 'list, perhaps,
Off-hand like - just as I
Was out of work - had sold his traps -
No other reason why.

Yes; quaint and curious war is!
You shoot a fellow down
You'd treat, if met where any bar is,
Or help to half a crown.

An August Midnight
A shaded lamp and a waving blind,
And the beat of a clock from a distant floor:
On this scene enter - winged, horned, and spined -
A longlegs, a moth, and a dumbledore;
While 'mid my page there idly stands
A sleepy fly, that rubs its hands

Thus meet we five, in this still place,
At this point of time, at this point in space.
My guests parade my new-penned ink,
Or bang at the lamp-glass, whirl, and sink.
"God's humblest, they!" I muse. Yet why?

They know Earth-secrets that know not I.

The Dead Man Walking
They hail me as one living,
But don't they know
That I have died of late years,
Untombed although?

I am but a shape that stands here,
A pulseless mould,
A pale past picture, screening
Ashes gone cold.

Not at a minute's warning,
Not in a loud hour,
For me ceased Time's enchantments
In hall and bower.

There was no tragic transit,
No catch of breath,
When silent seasons inched me
On to this death ...

A Troubadour-youth I rambled
With Life for lyre,
The beats of being raging
In me like fire.

But when I practised eyeing
The goal of men,
It iced me, and I perished
A little then.

When passed my friend, my kinsfolk,
Through the Last Door,
And left me standing bleakly,
I died yet more;

And when my Love's heart kindled
In hate of me,
Wherefore I knew not, died I
One more degree.

And if when I died fully
I cannot say,
And changed into the corpse-thing
I am to-day,

Yet is it that, though whiling
The time somehow

In walking, talking, smiling,
I live not now.

Lines On The Loss Of The "Titanic"
In a solitude of the sea
Deep from human vanity,
And the Pride of Life that planned her, stilly couches she.

Steel chambers, late the pyres
Of her salamandrine fires,
Cold currents thrid, and turn to rhythmic tidal lyres.

Over the mirrors meant
To glass the opulent
The sea-worm crawls - grotesque, slimed, dumb, indifferent.

Jewels in joy designed
To ravish the sensuous mind
Lie lightless, all their sparkles bleared and black and blind.

Dim moon-eyed fishes near
Gaze at the gilded gear
And query: "What does this vaingloriousness down here?"

Well: while was fashioning
This creature of cleaving wing,
The Immanent Will that stirs and urges everything

Prepared a sinister mate
For her - so gaily great
A Shape of Ice, for the time far and dissociate.

And as the smart ship grew
In stature, grace, and hue,
In shadowy silent distance grew the Iceberg too.

Alien they seemed to be;
No mortal eye could see
The intimate welding of their later history,

Or sign that they were bent
By paths coincident
On being anon twin halves of one august event,

Till the Spinner of the Years
Said "Now!" And each one hears,
And consummation comes, and jars two hemispheres.

Rome: The Vatican - Sala Delle Muse
I sat in the Muses' Hall at the mid of the day,

And it seemed to grow still, and the people to pass away,
And the chiselled shapes to combine in a haze of sun,
Till beside a Carrara column there gleamed forth One.

She was nor this nor that of those beings divine,
But each and the whole--an essence of all the Nine;
With tentative foot she neared to my halting-place,
A pensive smile on her sweet, small, marvellous face.

"Regarded so long, we render thee sad?" said she.
"Not you," sighed I, "but my own inconstancy!
I worship each and each; in the morning one,
And then, alas! another at sink of sun.

"To-day my soul clasps Form; but where is my troth
Of yesternight with Tune: can one cleave to both?"
"Be not perturbed," said she. "Though apart in fame,
As I and my sisters are one, those, too, are the same.

"But my loves go further--to Story, and Dance, and Hymn,
The lover of all in a sun-sweep is fool to whim -
Is swayed like a river-weed as the ripples run!"
"Nay, wight, thou sway'st not. These are but phases of one;

"And that one is I; and I am projected from thee,
One that out of thy brain and heart thou causest to be -
Extern to thee nothing. Grieve not, nor thyself becall,
Woo where thou wilt; and rejoice thou canst love at all!

Middle-Age Enthusiasms
To M. H.

We passed where flag and flower
Signalled a jocund throng;
We said: "Go to, the hour
Is apt!" - and joined the song;
And, kindling, laughed at life and care,
Although we knew no laugh lay there.

We walked where shy birds stood
Watching us, wonder-dumb;
Their friendship met our mood;
We cried: "We'll often come:
We'll come morn, noon, eve, everywhen!"
We doubted we should come again.

We joyed to see strange sheens
Leap from quaint leaves in shade;
A secret light of greens
They'd for their pleasure made.
We said: "We'll set such sorts as these!"

We knew with night the wish would cease.

"So sweet the place," we said,
"Its tacit tales so dear,
Our thoughts, when breath has sped,
Will meet and mingle here!"
"Words!" mused we. "Passed the mortal door,
Our thoughts will reach this nook no more."

Unknowing
When, soul in soul reflected,
We breathed an aethered air,
When we neglected
All things elsewhere,
And left the friendly friendless
To keep our love aglow,
We deemed it endless
We did not know!

When, by mad passion goaded,
We planned to hie away,
But, unforeboded,
The storm-shafts gray
So heavily down-pattered
That none could forthward go,
Our lives seemed shattered
We did not know!

When I found you, helpless lying,
And you waived my deep misprise,
And swore me, dying,
In phantom-guise
To wing to me when grieving,
And touch away my woe,
We kissed, believing...
--We did not know!

But though, your powers outreckoning,
You hold you dead and dumb,
Or scorn my beckoning,
And will not come;
And I say, "'Twere mood ungainly
To store her memory so:"
I say it vainly
I feel and know!

In Vision I Roamed
IN vision I roamed the flashing Firmament,
So fierce in blazon that the Night waxed wan,
As though with an awed sense of such ostent;

And as I thought my spirit ranged on and on

In footless traverse through ghast heights of sky,
To the last chambers of the monstrous Dome,
Where stars the brightest here to darkness die:
Then, any spot on our own Earth seemed Home!

And the sick grief that you were far away
Grew pleasant thankfulness that you were near,
Who might have been, set on some outstep sphere,
Less than a Want to me, as day by day
I lived unware, uncaring all that lay
Locked in that Universe taciturn and drear.

"I Have Lived With Shades"
I have lived with shades so long,
And talked to them so oft,
Since forth from cot and croft
I went mankind among,
That sometimes they
In their dim style
Will pause awhile
To hear my say;

And take me by the hand,
And lead me through their rooms
In the To-be, where Dooms
Half-wove and shapeless stand:
And show from there
The dwindled dust
And rot and rust
Of things that were.

"Now turn," spake they to me
One day: "Look whence we came,
And signify his name
Who gazes thence at thee."
"Nor name nor race
Know I, or can,"
I said, "Of man
So commonplace.

"He moves me not at all;
I note no ray or jot
Of rareness in his lot,
Or star exceptional.
Into the dim
Dead throngs around
He'll sink, nor sound
Be left of him."

"Yet," said they, "his frail speech,
Hath accents pitched like thine
Thy mould and his define
A likeness each to each -
But go! Deep pain
Alas, would be
His name to thee,
And told in vain!"

Memory And I

"O memory, where is now my youth,
Who used to say that life was truth?"

"I saw him in a crumbled cot
Beneath a tottering tree;
That he as phantom lingers there
Is only known to me."

"O Memory, where is now my joy,
Who lived with me in sweet employ?"

"I saw him in gaunt gardens lone,
Where laughter used to be;
That he as phantom wanders there
Is known to none but me."

"O Memory, where is now my hope,
Who charged with deeds my skill and scope?"

"I saw her in a tomb of tomes,
Where dreams are wont to be;
That she as spectre haunteth there
Is only known to me."

"O Memory, where is now my faith,
One time a champion, now a wraith?"

"I saw her in a ravaged aisle,
Bowed down on bended knee;
That her poor ghost outflickers there
Is known to none but me."
"O Memory, where is now my love,
That rayed me as a god above?"

"I saw him by an ageing shape
Where beauty used to be;
That his fond phantom lingers there
Is only known to me."

A Man (In Memory of H. of M.)
In Casterbridge there stood a noble pile,
Wrought with pilaster, bay, and balustrade
In tactful times when shrewd Eliza swayed.
On burgher, squire, and clown
It smiled the long street down for near a mile

But evil days beset that domicile;
The stately beauties of its roof and wall
Passed into sordid hands. Condemned to fall
Were cornice, quoin, and cove,
And all that art had wove in antique style.

Among the hired dismantlers entered there
One till the moment of his task untold.
When charged therewith he gazed, and answered bold:
"Be needy I or no,
I will not help lay low a house so fair!

"Hunger is hard. But since the terms be such
No wage, or labour stained with the disgrace
Of wrecking what our age cannot replace
To save its tasteless soul
I'll do without your dole. Life is not much!

Dismissed with sneers he backed his tools and went,
And wandered workless; for it seemed unwise
To close with one who dared to criticize
And carp on points of taste:
To work where they were placed rude men were meant.

Years whiled. He aged, sank, sickened, and was not:
And it was said, "A man intractable
And curst is gone." None sighed to hear his knell,
None sought his churchyard-place;
His name, his rugged face, were soon forgot.

The stones of that fair hall lie far and wide,
And but a few recall its ancient mould;
Yet when I pass the spot I long to hold
As truth what fancy saith:
"His protest lives where deathless things abide!"

Mute Opinion
I traversed a dominion
Whose spokesmen spake out strong
Their purpose and opinion
Through pulpit, press, and song.
I scarce had means to note there

A large-eyed few, and dumb,
Who thought not as those thought there
That stirred the heat and hum.

When, grown a Shade, beholding
That land in lifetime trode,
To learn if its unfolding
Fulfilled its clamoured code,
I saw, in web unbroken,
Its history outwrought
Not as the loud had spoken,
But as the mute had thought.

On An Invitation To The United States
My ardours for emprize nigh lost
Since Life has bared its bones to me,
I shrink to seek a modern coast
Whose riper times have yet to be;
Where the new regions claim them free
From that long drip of human tears
Which peoples old in tragedy
Have left upon the centuried years.

For, wonning in these ancient lands,
Enchased and lettered as a tomb,
And scored with prints of perished hands,
And chronicled with dates of doom,
Though my own Being bear no bloom
I trace the lives such scenes enshrine,
Give past exemplars present room,
And their experience count as mine.

The Tenant-For-Life
The sun said, watching my watering-pot
"Some morn you'll pass away;
These flowers and plants I parch up hot
Who'll water them that day?

"Those banks and beds whose shape your eye
Has planned in line so true,
New hands will change, unreasoning why
Such shape seemed best to you.

"Within your house will strangers sit,
And wonder how first it came;
They'll talk of their schemes for improving it,
And will not mention your name.

"They'll care not how, or when, or at what

You sighed, laughed, suffered here,
Though you feel more in an hour of the spot
Than they will feel in a year

"As I look on at you here, now,
Shall I look on at these;
But as to our old times, avow
No knowledge--hold my peace!

"O friend, it matters not, I say;
Bethink ye, I have shined
On nobler ones than you, and they
Are dead men out of mind!"

Afterwards
When the Present has latched its postern behind my tremulous stay,
And the May month flaps its glad green leaves like wings,
Delicate-filmed as new-spun silk, will the neighbours say,
"He was a man who used to notice such things"?

If it be in the dusk when, like an eyelid's soundless blink,
The dewfall-hawk comes crossing the shades to alight
Upon the wind-warped upland thorn, a gazer may think,
"To him this must have been a familiar sight."

If I pass during some nocturnal blackness, mothy and warm,
When the hedgehog travels furtively over the lawn,
One may say, "He strove that such innocent creatures should
come to no harm, But he could do little for them; and now he is gone."

If, when hearing that I have been stilled at last, they stand at
the door, Watching the full-starred heavens that winter sees,
Will this thought rise on those who will meet my face no more,
"He was one who had an eye for such mysteries"?

And will any say when my bell of quittance is heard in the gloom,
And a crossing breeze cuts a pause in its outrollings,
Till they rise again, as they were a new bell's boom,
"He hears it not now, but used to notice such things?"

During Wind And Rain
They sing their dearest songs
He, she, all of them yea,
Treble and tenor and bass,
And one to play;
With the candles mooning each face
Ah, no; the years O!
How the sick leaves reel down in throngs!

They clear the creeping moss
Elders and juniors aye,
Making the pathways neat
And the garden gay;
And they build a shady seat
Ah, no; the years, the years;
See, the white storm-birds wing across!

They are blithely breakfasting all
Men and maidens yea,
Under the summer tree,
With a glimpse of the bay,
While pet fowl come to the knee
Ah, no; the years O!
And the rotten rose is ript from the wall.

They change to a high new house,
He, she, all of them aye,
Clocks and carpets and chairs
On the lawn all day,
And brightest things that are theirs
Ah, no; the years, the years;
Down their carved names the rain-drop ploughs.

The Seasons of Her Year
Winter is white on turf and tree,
And birds are fled;
But summer songsters pipe to me,
And petals spread,
For what I dreamt of secretly
His lips have said!

O 'tis a fine May morn, they say,
And blooms have blown;
But wild and wintry is my day,
My birds make moan;
For he who vowed leaves me to pay
Alone--alone!

Heredity
I am the family face;
Flesh perishes, I live on,
Projecting trait and trace
Through time to times anon,
And leaping from place to place
Over oblivion.

The years-heired feature that can
In curve and voice and eye

Despise the human span
Of durance -- that is I;
The eternal thing in man,
That heeds no call to die

He Never Expected Much
Well, World, you have kept faith with me,
Kept faith with me;
Upon the whole you have proved to be
Much as you said you were.
Since as a child I used to lie
Upon the leaze and watch the sky,
Never, I own, expected I
That life would all be fair.

'Twas then you said, and since have said,
Times since have said,
In that mysterious voice you shed
From clouds and hills around:
"Many have loved me desperately,
Many with smooth serenity,
While some have shown contempt of me
Till they dropped underground.

"I do not promise overmuch,
Child; overmuch;
Just neutral-tinted haps and such,"
You said to minds like mine.
Wise warning for your credit's sake!
Which I for one failed not to take,
And hence could stem such strain and ache
As each year might assign.

I Said To Love
I said to Love,
"It is not now as in old days
When men adored thee and thy ways
All else above;
Named thee the Boy, the Bright, the One
Who spread a heaven beneath the sun,"
I said to Love.

I said to him,
"We now know more of thee than then;
We were but weak in judgment when,
With hearts abrim,
We clamoured thee that thou would'st please
Inflict on us thine agonies,"
I said to him.

I said to Love,
"Thou art not young, thou art not fair,
No elfin darts, no cherub air,
Nor swan, nor dove
Are thine; but features pitiless,
And iron daggers of distress,"
I said to Love.

"Depart then, Love!
Man's race shall perish, threatenest thou,
WIthout thy kindling coupling-vow?
The age to come the man of now
Know nothing of?
We fear not such a threat from thee;
We are too old in apathy!
Mankind shall cease
So let it be,"
I said to Love.

I Look Into My Glass
I look into my glass,
And view my wasting skin,
And say, "Would God it came to pass
My heart had shrunk as thin!"

For then, I, undistrest
By hearts grown cold to me,
Could lonely wait my endless rest
With equanimity.

But Time, to make me grieve,
Part steals, lets part abide;
And shakes this fragile frame at eve
With throbbings of noontide.

The Subalterns
"Poor wanderer," said the leaden sky,
"I fain would lighten thee,
But there are laws in force on high
Which say it must not be."

"I would not freeze thee, shorn one," cried
The North, "knew I but how
To warm my breath, to slack my stride;
But I am ruled as thou."

"To-morrow I attack thee, wight,"
Said Sickness. "Yet I swear

I bear thy little ark no spite,
But am bid enter there."

"Come hither, Son," I heard Death say;
"I did not will a grave
Should end thy pilgrimage to-day,
But I, too, am a slave!"

We smiled upon each other then,
And life to me had less
Of that fell look it wore ere when
They owned their passiveness.

She At His Funeral
They bear him to his resting-place
In slow procession sweeping by;
I follow at a stranger's space;
His kindred they, his sweetheart I.
Unchanged my gown of garish dye,
Though sable-sad is their attire;
But they stand round with griefless eye,
Whilst my regret consumes like fire!

The Church-Builder
The church flings forth a battled shade
Over the moon-blanched sward:
The church; my gift; whereto I paid
My all in hand and hoard;
Lavished my gains
With stintless pains
To glorify the Lord.

I squared the broad foundations in
Of ashlared masonry;
I moulded mullions thick and thin,
Hewed fillet and ogee;
I circleted
Each sculptured head
With nimb and canopy.

I called in many a craftsmaster
To fix emblazoned glass,
To figure Cross and Sepulchure
On dossal, boss, and brass.
My gold all spent,
My jewels went
To gem the cups of Mass.

I borrowed deep to carve the screen

And raise the ivoried Rood;
I parted with my small demesne
To make my owings good.
Heir-looms unpriced
I sacrificed,
Until debt-free I stood.

So closed the task. "Deathless the Creed
Here substanced!" said my soul:
"I heard me bidden to this deed,
And straight obeyed the call.
Illume this fane,
That not in vain
I build it, Lord of all!"

But, as it chanced me, then and there
Did dire misfortunes burst;
My home went waste for lack of care,
My sons rebelled and curst;
Till I confessed
That aims the best
Were looking like the worst.

Enkindled by my votive work
No burnng faith I find;
The deeper thinkers sneer and smirk,
And give my toil no mind;
From nod and wink
I read they think
That I am fool and blind.

My gift to God seems futile, quite;
The world moves as erstwhile;
And powerful Wrong on feeble Right
Tramples in olden style.
My faith burns down,
I see no crown;
But Cares, and Griefs, and Guile.

So now, the remedy? Yea, this:
I gently swing the door
Here, of my fane--no soul to wis
And cross the patterned floor
To the rood-screen
That stands between
The nave and inner chore.

The rich red windows dim the moon,
But little light need I;
I mount the prie-dieu, lately hewn
From woods of rarest dye;

Then from below
My garment, so,
I draw this cord, and tie

One end thereof around the beam
Midway 'twixt Cross and truss:
I noose the nethermost extreme,
And in ten seconds thus
I journey hence
To that land whence
No rumour reaches us.

Well: Here at morn they'll light on one
Dangling in mockery
Of what he spent his substance on
Blindly and uselessly!
"He might," they'll say,
"Have built, some way,
A cheaper gallows-tree!"

Men Who March Away
Song of the Soldiers

What of the faith and fire within us
Men who march away
Ere the barn-cocks say
Night is growing gray,
To hazards whence no tears can win us;
What of the faith and fire within us
Men who march away!

Is it a purblind prank, O think you,
Friend with the musing eye
Who watch us stepping by,
With doubt and dolorous sigh?
Can much pondering so hoodwink you?
Is it a purblind prank, O think you,
Friend with the musing eye?

Nay. We see well what we are doing,
Though some may not see
Dalliers as they be
England's need are we;
Her distress would leave us rueing:
Nay. We well see what we are doing,
Though some may not see!

In our heart of hearts believing
Victory crowns the just,
And that braggarts must

Surely bite the dust,
Press we to the field ungrieving,
In our heart of hearts believing
Victory crowns the just.

Hence the faith and fire within us
Men who march away
Ere the barn-cocks say
Night is growing gray,
To hazards whence no tears can win us;
Hence the faith and fire within us
Men who march away.

She, To Him
When you shall see me lined by tool of Time,
My lauded beauties carried off from me,
My eyes no longer stars as in their prime,
My name forgot of Maiden Fair and Free;

When in your being heart concedes to mind,
And judgment, though you scarce its process know,
Recalls the excellencies I once enshrined,
And you are irked that they have withered so:

Remembering that with me lies not the blame,
That Sportsman Time but rears his brood to kill,
Knowing me in my soul the very same
One who would die to spare you touch of ill!
Will you not grant to old affection's claim
The hand of friendship down Life's sunless hill?

To An Unborn Pauper Child
Breathe not, hid Heart: cease silently,
And though thy birth-hour beckons thee,
Sleep the long sleep:
The Doomsters heap
Travails and teens around us here,
And Time-Wraiths turn our songsingings to fear.

Hark, how the peoples surge and sigh,
And laughters fail, and greetings die;
Hopes dwindle; yea,
Faiths waste away,
Affections and enthusiasms numb:
Thou canst not mend these things if thou dost come.

Had I the ear of wombed souls
Ere their terrestrial chart unrolls,
And thou wert free

To cease, or be,
Then would I tell thee all I know,
And put it to thee: Wilt thou take Life so?

Vain vow! No hint of mine may hence
To theeward fly: to thy locked sense
Explain none can
Life's pending plan:
Thou wilt thy ignorant entry make
Though skies spout fire and blood and nations quake.

Fain would I, dear, find some shut plot
Of earth's wide wold for thee, where not
One tear, one qualm,
Should break the calm.
No man can change the common lot to rare.

Must come and bide. And such are we
Unreasoning, sanguine, visionary
That I can hope
Health, love, friends, scope
In full for thee; can dream thou'lt find
Joys seldom yet attained by humankind!

The To-Be-Forgotten
I heard a small sad sound,
And stood awhile among the tombs around:
"Wherefore, old friends," said I, "are you distrest,
Now, screened from life's unrest?"

"O not at being here;
But that our future second death is near;
When, with the living, memory of us numbs,
And blank oblivion comes!

"These, our sped ancestry,
Lie here embraced by deeper death than we;
Nor shape nor thought of theirs can you descry
With keenest backward eye.

"They count as quite forgot;
They are as men who have existed not;
Theirs is a loss past loss of fitful breath;
It is the second death.

"We here, as yet, each day
Are blest with dear recall; as yet, can say
We hold in some soul loved continuance
Of shape and voice and glance.

"But what has been will be
First memory, then oblivion's swallowing sea;
Like men foregone, shall we merge into those
Whose story no one knows.

"For which of us could hope
To show in life that world-awakening scope
Granted the few whose memory none lets die,
But all men magnify?

"We were but Fortune's sport;
Things true, things lovely, things of good report
We neither shunned nor sought ... We see our bourne,
And seeing it we mourn."

In A Museum
Here's the mould of a musical bird long passed from light,
Which over the earth before man came was winging;
There's a contralto voice I heard last night,
That lodges with me still in its sweet singing.

Such a dream is Time that the coo of this ancient bird
Has perished not, but is blent, or will be blending
Mid visionless wilds of space with the voice that I heard,
In the full-fuged song of the universe unending.

A Confession To A Friend In Trouble
Your troubles shrink not, though I feel them less
Here, far away, than when I tarried near;
I even smile old smiles, with listlessness
Yet smiles they are, not ghastly mockeries mere.

A thought too strange to house within my brain
Haunting its outer precincts I discern:
That I will not show zeal again to learn
Your griefs, and, sharing them, renew my pain

It goes, like murky bird or buccaneer
That shapes its lawless figure on the main,
And each new impulse tends to make outflee
The unseemly instinct that had lodgment here;
Yet, comrade old, can bitterer knowledge be
Than that, though banned, such instinct was in me!

Shelley's Skylark (The neighbourhood of Leghorn: March)
Somewhere afield here something lies
In Earth's oblivious eyeless trust
That moved a poet to prophecies

A pinch of unseen, unguarded dust

The dust of the lark that Shelley heard,
And made immortal through times to be;
Though it only lived like another bird,
And knew not its immortality.

Lived its meek life; then, one day, fell
A little ball of feather and bone;
And how it perished, when piped farewell,
And where it wastes, are alike unknown.

Maybe it rests in the loam I view,
Maybe it throbs in a myrtle's green,
Maybe it sleeps in the coming hue
Of a grape on the slopes of yon inland scene.

Go find it, faeries, go and find
That tiny pinch of priceless dust,
And bring a casket silver-lined,
And framed of gold that gems encrust;

And we will lay it safe therein,
And consecrate it to endless time;
For it inspired a bard to win
Ecstatic heights in thought and rhyme.

www.ingramcontent.com/pod-product-compliance
Lightning Source LLC
Chambersburg PA
CBHW061317040426
42444CB00010B/2689